THE IRS SCANDAL, which has riveted the public's attention for months, is much larger and much more complex than the Obama administration wants to acknowledge. The targeting of conservative groups by the IRS, the most serious of the Obamagate scandals, is no more the responsibility of "rogue agents in Cincinnati" than the massacre in Benghazi is of a rogue videographer. This scandal is rather the result of a strategy set forth by the White House and its "progressive" allies in the Washington bureaucracy and policy apparatus to silence conservative groups and individuals deemed to be a political threat to the current administration and to advance left-wing campaign finance laws. While President Obama called this massive abuse of the IRS "inexcusable," his administration has found plenty of excuses not to "get to the bottom of it," as his press secretary Jay Carney initially promised it would. In the first flurry of damage control, Obama told the media he had instructed Treasury Secretary Jacob Lew to investigate, but Obama left

out the probability that Lew learned of the targeting – and perhaps coordinated it – in May 2012, when he was the president's chief of staff.

Conservatives looking for empirical evidence of what they knew by experience was happening to them as a result of IRS "scrutiny" placed hope in the report issued by J. Russell George, the Treasury Department

---

It is profoundly against the American grain that the federal tax code should have become a fun park for the powerful.

---

inspector general for tax administration, at about the time the scandal erupted. This report indeed authenticated the focus on conservative groups and the use of *Tea Party, patriot, 9/12,* and similar search terms. But we still don't know the exact criteria by which the IRS constructed its "be on the lookout" (BOLO) list, the fulcrum used to give groups excessive screening. Nor is there any indication that the report used the agency's extensive data-mining capacity to investigate the abusive and illegitimate targeting. Such deficits give the report the feel of damage control, despite its revelations, rather than a rigorous attempt to get to the bottom of things.

As late as June 2013, long after Congress began investigating the scandal that the administration promised was a mistake of the past, pro-life groups were still being badgered for information about their anti-abortion activities. "We've had three more groups come to us that have had problems with the IRS – some very recent, some current or still pending," Peter Breen, senior counsel at the Thomas More Society – which represents pro-life groups targeted by the IRS – told the *Daily Caller*. "It's continuing, and it needs to be addressed."

In an August 2013 closed-door session of the House Ways and Means Committee, an unidentified IRS agent testified that Tea Party groups were still being forced into special "secondary screening" because the IRS still hasn't come up with new guidelines for granting tax-exempt status that guarantee an apolitical process. Meanwhile, months after the FBI announced that it would launch an investigation into the IRS's targeting of conservative groups, these groups and their legal representatives are still waiting to hear from the bureau.

Rather than being cured, this disease is at best in remission, as the House Oversight Committee, led by Representative Darrell Issa, tries to discern what the IRS did, to whom, and for how long. But this much is already apparent: a timeline extrapolated from White House visitor logs shows that the Obama administration has been dishonest about nearly every facet of the scandal, in which an archetypal pattern of response can be seen. First, plead ignorance. (If the president isn't in the loop, he can't be held accountable.) Next, offer a plausible story that involves low-level employees, to be floated by sympathetic bloggers and journalists. (It helps if the talking points are provided to these journalists in closed-door meetings.) Finally, when caught lying, slow-walk any investigation and promote anyone associated with the scandal, so it will be tougher for Congress to compel them to testify.

A Crooked Path

Then-Treasury Secretary Timothy Geithner met with then-IRS Commissioner Douglas Schulman, then-White House Chief of Staff Lew, and President Obama on May 10, 2012. The timing is significant because the president claimed that he didn't learn of the targeting until almost exactly a year later, in May 2013, when he saw a story about it on television, although Issa had repeatedly expressed concerns that the IRS was unfairly targeting Tea Party groups.

A flurry of activity after this White House meeting suggests an effort to get everyone on the same page over the next year. On June 4, 2012, Deputy Treasury Secretary Neal Wolin met with J. Russell George, the IRS inspector general for tax administration, who was already working on the report mentioned above in response to Issa's complaints, about ongoing audits being pursued by the agency's watchdog office. On September 10, Geithner himself met with George. On September 19, Steven Miller – who had by then replaced Schulman as IRS commissioner – met again with Geithner. On September 27, Geithner met with Deputy Secretary Wolin and later with Shulman, who in testimony before the House in March 2012 had gone out of his way to deny that any extra scrutiny was being given to conservative groups. The purpose of this meeting was primarily to plan the implementation of Obamacare, whose protection, we now see, was deemed important enough to justify IRS intimidation of groups opposing it.

Although White House Chief Counsel Kathryn Ruemmler claimed to have learned about the IRS auditing of conservative groups only in April 2013, she had three unprecedented one-on-one meetings in 2012 with the Treasury Department's chief lawyer, Christopher J. Meade, who had known about the report Inspector General George had begun working on since at least June of that year. Meade met with Ruemmler on September 27, December 11, and December 13, according to White House visitor records. The two had never met one-on-one before.

The meetings served one purpose – to alert all the relevant administration officials about the talking points for the forthcoming report George was about to deliver. In anticipation of this event, the White House battened down the hatches. Shulman and Geithner resigned, putting them, for all practical considerations, beyond the reach of Congress. Lew, the new Treasury secretary, could avoid testimony by having the president claim executive privilege, given his past job as White House chief of staff.

Cindy Thomas, the IRS official who headed the exempt-organizations office in the Cincinnati branch at the time conservative groups applying for tax-exempt status were targeted, was promoted. Daniel Werfel, principal deputy

IRS commissioner, was slated to leave as of August 2013, but not before slowing the investigation and taking the bullet from Congress.

Lois Lerner – the woman at the center of the scandal – continued to hold her job as director of the tax-exempt organizations division, despite IRS regulations stating that if an IRS employee receives a request from elsewhere in the Executive Branch that could be construed as an abuse or a violation of the law, the employee must report it or face prosecution. It has emerged that Lerner, who has a long history of liberal activism and selective leaking of tax information to her old colleagues at the Federal Election Commission, corresponded about the targeting using her personal e-mail address so as to avoid scrutiny. Lerner took an early retirement in late September and received her full pension. Her lawyer was working out a deal with congressional investigators as this went to press.

* * *

The targeting of conservative groups was real – a threat to them and to our ability to speak and act freely.

Who Collects the Taxes Matters Most

The U.S. was, of course, founded on a tax revolt. It is profoundly against the American grain that the federal tax code should have become a fun park for the powerful. Its staggering complexity – more than 75,000 pages and counting – has offered plenty of opportunity for inside players to avoid paying the taxes they owe. Both Barack Obama's Treasury secretaries – Timothy Geithner and Jacob Lew – have had tax troubles resulting from this temptation, with Geithner owing more than $34,000 in back taxes and Lew hiding his assets offshore in the Cayman Islands.

Using one's contacts for personal gain has nonetheless become a reflexive gesture for insiders. Hillary Clinton's former chief of staff Huma Abedin, for instance, has moonlighted as a consultant to firms run by Clinton aides, to the Clinton Global Initiative, and even to the Clintons personally without disclosing any of it, according to the *New York Times*. She is by no means the only representative of a "government" class that trades on its access to information for personal and political profit. From congressmen of both political parties who make personal use of material revealed during committee hearings to bureaucrats who leak confidential and sensitive material to their allies in the press, the problem is as commonplace as it is damaging. The technology developed by the growing ranks (and class) of federal contractors further enables their self-serving behavior.

The problem is far greater than personal venality when the organizations known as 501(c)(3) and 501(c)(4), which are at the heart of this scandal, are involved. These nonprofit organizations use individuals' donations – in some cases, tax-deductible ones – to engage in charitable and educational activity and political advocacy, which is the opposite side of its coin, and they have the ability to influence the issues of the day. These organizations might have been established with an eye toward promoting social welfare, but particularly since the advent of campaign-finance reform, they have become an avenue of political advocacy by other means, all the more powerful because they are tax exempt and offer theoretical anonymity to donors.

No wonder then that the stakes are so high in the IRS scandal. And no wonder that the Obama administration worked so desperately to create three persistent myths to try to make it disappear: that only unauthorized employees were involved; that it began under a conservative Republican official; and that progressive groups were also targeted.

The "rogue agents in Cincinnati" narrative had problems from the beginning. If it were true that only a handful of freelancing analysts were responsible for the targeting of conservative groups, why did George's report mention the involvement of Washington-based IRS "guidance specialists" and "technical specialists"? Why, again according to page 29 of that report, did the program manager of the Cincinnati office answer to *six* different Washington superiors?

Washington-based IRS lawyer Carter C. Hull oversaw the Cincinnati office's targeting of Tea Party groups and even provided the officials there an intimidating sample request for information that he had sent to the Albuquerque Tea Party. The employees in Cincinnati complied with Hall's orders but refused to take the fall later on. "I was essentially a front person because I had no autonomy or no authority to act on [applications] without Carter Hull's influence or input," one supposedly rogue employee told congressional investigators.

It soon emerged that in addition to the Cincinnati office, at least four other IRS offices targeted conservatives: Washington, D.C.; Chicago;

and Laguna Niguel and El Monte in California.

In a clumsy attempt at blame shifting, Representative Elijah Cummings, the top Democrat on the House Oversight Committee, attempted to defend the administration during Congressional hearings by claiming that it was actually a lone "conservative Republican" from the Bush years who had initiated the targeting. "That's ridiculous. [Cummings' claim] is nonsense," Jay Sekulow, chief counsel of the American Center for Law and Justice and an attorney representing over 40 Tea Party groups in a class-action lawsuit, told the *Daily Caller*. This lone Republican was never convincingly identified. But, as Sekulow says, "We know that Lois Lerner was sending letters to Tea Party groups from Washington."

As director of the tax-exempt organizations division, Lerner has a long history of selective targeting. She has dragged her heels or looked the other way when left-wing groups such as the Humane Society admitted to pursuing an openly political campaign that directly violates 501(c)(3) rules. (Interestingly enough, Lois

Lerner was once a member of the Humane Society. Joyce Doria, a member of the group's national council since 2011, was also a senior vice president and senior partner at Booz Allen Hamilton, one of the larger data-mining companies headquartered in Virginia.) One nonprofit, Justice Through Music, still has its tax-exempt status despite being headed by Brett Kimberlin, a left-wing domestic terrorist and bomber who employed a convicted child molester at his nonprofit to harass his estranged wife. Lerner is like other IRS officials in that she has learned from the organization's institutional culture that high officials are free to use contacts in the media, government, and nonprofit world to reward friends as well as harass political opponents and silence political speech with which they disagree.

The most desperate gambit on the part of the administration's defenders in the IRS scandal has been pushed by those like the *New York Times* editors, who have tried to portray the agency as an equal-opportunity oppressor, arguing that because the word *progressive* appeared on the infamous BOLO list of key terms, along with *Tea Party* and *patriot,* such groups were also targeted with equal malignity.

But the Treasury Department inspector general's letter to congressional Democrats in June 2013 revealed that only six progressive groups were selected for additional scrutiny regarding their tax-exempt status, compared with 292 conservative organizations. Only 30 percent of groups with the word *progressive* in their name were selected for special scrutiny, but 100 percent of groups with the words *Tea Party, patriot,* or *9/12* were targeted. To date, no progressive group has claimed that it was improperly singled out for heightened scrutiny.

The unholy alliance between Big Data and Big Government is what gives this scandal the feel of something unprecedented.

The targeting of conservative groups was real – a threat to them and to our ability to speak and act freely. It came about for two reasons: the administration was desperate to stop grassroots opposition to Obamacare, and progressives were desperate to retain political advantages they had enjoyed until the *Citizens United v. Federal Election Commission* (2010) decision by the Supreme Court weakened campaign-finance laws. Indeed emails released in September from Lois Lerner show disdain for the court ruling and hope that the "the FEC will save the day" from the Tea Party. "Tea Party matter very dangerous. This could be the vehicle to go to court on the issue over whether Citizen's United overturning the ban on corporate spending applies to tax exempt rules," she wrote on February 11 to IRS executive and Obama donor Holly Paz.

The targeting of conservatives was planned and assisted by some of the most powerful lawyers in the country, among them IRS chief counsel William Wilkins, who met with Obama two days before the agency set up the criteria for going after the Tea Party groups (and who as a private attorney had successfully represented Obama's then-pastor Jeremiah Wright during his legal battle to save his church's tax-exempt status). Also involved was Douglas Shulman, who as IRS commissioner had met with Obama 157 times (his predecessor had met with the president just once) and whose wife, Susan Anderson, works for Public Campaign, a left-wing group that wants what it calls "sweeping campaign reform."

Campaign-finance reform, of course, is campaign control. What liberal activists were not able to secure through campaign-finance laws, the Federal Election Commission, and the ill-fated DISCLOSE Act in response to the Supreme Court's *Citizens United* decision, they have sought to achieve through the IRS, a bureaucracy committed to the ideological project of increasing the size and scope of government power.

* * *

How did this nightmare take shape? The answer is being slowly extracted from the layers of self-protective deniability with which the IRS surrounds itself. But we know that the unholy alliance between Big Data and Big Government is what gives this scandal the feel of something unprecedented.

Enhanced information technology after 9/11 meant that more data was being generated than ever before. The USA Patriot Act and subsequent legislation meant that this information was being shared between enabled executive agencies to a degree previously unimaginable. Unable to deal with the staggering amount of data that it now produced, the government accelerated the outsourcing of analysis to federal contractors. Programs like the National Security Agency's contentious PRISM, which monitors phone-call logs kept by telecommunications companies; and Aladdin, which archives all online video content, were created to help law-enforcement agencies find patterns in seemingly random data sets. Regulation by regulation, all the old firewalls within agencies and between them began to blur or were eliminated entirely.

By 2002, the IRS was reorganizing and restructuring the technology of four of its computer data systems as part of a government-wide response to the 9/11 attacks. One of those efforts led to the Tax Exempt Determination System (TEDS), technology that in effect allowed the IRS to troll tax-exempt organizations' applications for terms like *Tea Party* and opened the door for the kind of targeting we are hearing about now. Once that door opened, *Tea Party*, *patriot*, and other terms became the basis for the BOLO list.

Shared data made government agencies more supple in their use of information and better able to connect the dots that determined national security. But opening access to data came at a price: someone like Private Bradley Manning could now easily download data from diplomatic cables that had nothing to do with his unit or its mission and send them off to WikiLeaks.

As the various arms of government compiled more and more data, the sheer magnitude became overwhelming. So agencies began sending it, bit by bit and byte by byte, to data-mining firms such as Palantir and i2.

The IRS joined in this process, which amounted to a massive data-privatization goal. In 2004, in fact, it was chastised by the Government Accountability Office for not "giving meaningful consideration to other contractors" before awarding 36 of the 37 technology-providing tasks to Booz Allen Hamilton, where Edward Snowden worked before stealing sensitive NSA information. (In the late 2000s, Joyce Doria, a former senior VP and senior partner at Booz Allen Hamilton, was the organization's officer in charge of the restructuring of the IRS. "Under the direction of Ms. Doria, the Booz Allen team has been fundamentally transforming the IRS culture, completing a major organization restructuring, implementing a strategic management system to guide the Agency's future work, and changing the organization's approach to teamwork, communication, decision-making, and leadership," read a website for a company Doria later joined. She remained an elected member of the Booz Allen board of directors.)

With new information and enhanced abilities to deploy that information came new power for the IRS. The targeting of conservative groups is one example of its new reach into the body politic. Its coming role in Americans' health care decisions is another. In fact, the two have always been intimately connected. Sarah Hall Ingram, one of the officials tasked with helping the IRS implement Obamacare, has logged 165 meetings with White House officials since 2011 and may have been involved in the political targeting as well.

The IRS will have access to a huge volume of personal medical records under Obamacare when it is fully implemented, but the poor job it has done of safeguarding the data it already has gives pause. In March 2011, the

IRS seized 60 million medical records from a California health care provider while its agents were executing a warrant for a former employee's financial records, a blatant violation of the Health Insurance Portability and Accountability Act. In another instance, the agency admitted to unwittingly releasing thousands of Social Security numbers. When it comes to data, even information that it doesn't plan to use against targeted organizations, the IRS appears all too often to be the gang that couldn't shoot straight.

Doubling Down on Double Standards

If there is to be light at the end of the targeting scandal, it will likely have to be shone by Congress, although its Democratic members will resist the illumination because so much of the left's agenda, especially Obamacare, requires an IRS with unfettered access to personal data. But the IRS knows that while Congresses come and go, the agency is forever. Indeed, the contempt it has always had for Congress is breathtaking. A 1991 survey of 800 IRS executives and managers by the nonprofit Josephson Institute of Ethics found that three-quarters of them felt entitled to deceive or to lie when testifying before a congressional committee. Small wonder, then, that in the matter at hand, Lois Lerner pleaded the Fifth Amendment at the same time that she loudly insisted she had done nothing wrong, broken no laws, and followed all IRS rules. No act more symbolizes the implacable arrogance of an imperial institution or the roadblocks in the way of ferreting out the truth about the scandal.

A glaring example of double standards in the enforcement of the tax code – particularly striking when set against the backdrop of the targeting of conservative organizations – is that of the Barack H. Obama Foundation, run by Malik Obama, the president's half-brother. (To this day, Malik Obama proudly hangs a picture in his office of himself, circa 1990, with the late Libyan dictator Muammar Gaddafi. Malik Obama once dismissed Gaddafi's slaughter of his own people as no different from Israel's treatment of the Palestinians and even dedicated his book, *Barack Obama Sr.: The Rise and Life of a True African Scholar*, to him.) Malik's charity reported having received only $25,000 over a three-year period, although Malik himself bragged about how he had received $250,000, much of it from his friends in the Middle East.

The *New York Post* reported in May 2011 that this foundation had been operating for years without a tax-exempt status. An officer of the foundation candidly admitted that the organization hadn't been able "to find someone with the expertise" to apply for a tax exemption. But then the Barack H. Obama Foundation began what for other organizations has been a grueling application process and sailed through it in a couple of weeks. Lerner granted the organization a 501(c)(3) determination and even gave it a retroactive tax exemption dating back to December 2008.

At the same time that Lerner was giving a pass to Malik Obama, however, the IRS was

---

With new information and enhanced abilities to deploy that information came new power for the IRS. The targeting of conservative groups is one example of its new reach into the body politic.

---

sending letters demanding conservative groups' training materials; recommended reading lists; personal information on donors, staff, and interns; and even the contents of a religious group's prayers, while holding up its nonprofit status. This was a far cry from then-IRS Commissioner Steven T. Miller's October 22, 2007, guarantee to prospective applicants for nonprofit status that the IRS's "job is not to overburden you with eccentric, nit-picking, nonsensical rules."

During the Lerner regime, however, compliance for some was made all but impossible, thereby slowing down the legitimate activity of groups such as the Tea Party, at the same time that information was demanded on donors, finances, staff records, etc., that could be used to damage the targeted group by being leaked at a later date.

A Legacy of Intimidation

The IRS, founded in 1913 with the establishment of the federal income tax, was a unique creation in American history – immune from the rules that restrained other government institutions and chartered to intrude into private lives with impunity. Rather than the usual presumption of innocence that Americans expected in proceedings against them, taxpayers deemed delinquent by the IRS were assumed guilty until they proved otherwise. Alone among the citizens of industrialized countries, Americans are compelled to file an income-tax return regardless of where they reside in the world. Under Obama, the IRS has pursued Americans living abroad through private banks, leading to a sixfold increase in audits of 6 million Americans living abroad. Such a sword of Damocles has contributed to an alarming trend: 1,810 of these Americans renounced their citizenship during the first half of 2013, compared with 235 five years earlier in all of 2008.

Keeping on top of the sheer number of returns, many of them forbiddingly complex, has always bedeviled IRS officers. Even more punishingly, they have also had to deal with the usually tacit – but sometimes explicit (as in the case of the current scandal) – demands of the organization's political appointees that all their powers of investigation, harassment, and imprisonment were to be used for political purposes.

Such activity is commonly thought to have begun with Richard Nixon, but Franklin D. Roosevelt was there long before him. Godfather of the modern IRS, FDR thought nothing of targeting political enemies with the clear intent of breaking opposition figures such as anti-New Deal publishers Robert McCormick (owner of the *Chicago Tribune*), Moses Annenberg (owner of the *Philadelphia Inquirer*), and most of all Andrew Mellon, whom the president believed represented "the master mind among the malefactors of great wealth." Even after the IRS cleared Mellon of tax fraud, Roosevelt continued to press the case against him until Mellon died and was therefore out of Roosevelt's and the Justice Department's jurisdiction.

"In almost every administration since the IRS's inception the information and power of the tax agency have been mobilized for explicitly political purposes," writes David Burnham, author of *A Law Unto Itself: The IRS and the Abuse of Power* (1990). Richard Nixon's "Enemies List" became a national fear as well as a symbol of his paranoid presidency, but apparently the only person who was audited improperly was the *Washington Post*'s attorney Edward Bennett Williams. While the IRS's Special Services staff was alleged to have "compiled information on more than 1,000 institutions and 4,000 individuals," Nixon's effort to make the IRS a "politically pliable" agency was beyond his reach, as Stanley Kutler writes in *The Wars of Watergate.* The IRS remained what it had been long before Watergate – a "monstrous bureaucracy … dominated and controlled by Democrats."

However much Nixon may have fantasized about making the IRS into a reliable attack dog against his opponents, nothing he accomplished approaches the extent of the current IRS scandal, which began to develop soon after Obama's election, according to Cleta Mitchell, a partner at the prestigious Foley & Lardner law firm and one of a handful of national experts on the laws regulating nonprofits. In a video interview with Power Line's Scott Johnson, Mitchell says that she began to notice a dramatic change in the treatment of conservative organizations as early as 2009. Before, getting approval for nonprofit status took three to five weeks. Now it began to take months, which dragged into years.

One of the most flagrant examples was a

client of Mitchell's who wanted to form a nonprofit to research and publicize information about the dangers of the Affordable Care Act. This client filed an application in November 2009 and by June 2010 had heard nothing. Mitchell called the Washington office of the IRS and was given the runaround. It wasn't until nearly two years later, in the spring of 2012, that her client heard from the agency – with a letter demanding answers to hundreds of questions about the organization's donors, its political outlook, and its prospective activities.

"The IRS has lied consistently …" Mitchell says. "There was a concerted effort … to target conservative organizations. And that was a culture, and it emanated from the very highest reaches of authority in Washington, from the White House to members of Congress that [wanted] bad things to happen to conservative organizations and Tea Party groups."

In addition to slow-walking applications and inundating prospective nonprofits with intrusive questions that put its confidential relationship with donors at risk, the IRS was willing to take the intimidation to another level. Mitchell gives the nightmare example of another client – Catherine Engelbrecht of True the Vote, a Texas organization working against voter fraud. When Engelbrecht's application for nonprofit status was ignored, Mitchell sued the IRS. Soon after, the tax returns of Engelbrecht and her husband were audited. So was the husband's business, a small manufacturing firm outside Houston. It was visited by OSHA and EPA inspectors looking for violations. In addition, Engelbrecht was visited by the FBI on seven separate occasions.

"I don't believe in coincidences," Mitchell says. "I think the reason Catherine Engelbrecht and True the Vote were singled out is because she represents a huge threat to the left because of her commitment to train thousands of people nationwide as poll watchers."

Full Disclosure

The example of Engelbrecht is particularly daunting, but a cognate process of intimidation – the release of confidential tax informa-

Rather than the usual presumption of innocence that Americans expected in proceedings against them, taxpayers deemed delinquent by the IRS were assumed guilty until they proved otherwise.

tion by leftist groups with strong ties to the White House – has become commonplace in the past six years. Joel Gilbert, a filmmaker who made *Dreams from My Real Father,* a successful film posing questions about Barack Obama's parentage, had his personal banking information disclosed by Seth Rosenfeld, an operative with the George Soros-funded Center for Investigative Reporting. "Rosenfeld contacted me and my donors with confidential banking account information of every one of my investors and called me and detailed their exact wire transfer and check amounts," Gilbert says. "He would pose as relatives or as old friends of my donors and try to find out if they had donated to the Romney for President campaign. Sometimes he would pretend to be a representative of the Romney campaign and asked if they knew other investors or if they supported other conservative organizations. Some of my investors were spooked and decided not to participate, which was the point."

In March 2012, the National Organization for Marriage (NOM) also had its confidential tax information released to the public by another Soros-connected group, the Human Rights Campaign (HRC). The HRC subsequently put the leaked information, including a list of NOM donors, on its website. The information was picked up by the popular *Huffington Post* website and went viral.

NOM discovered that the information the Human Rights Campaign released had come directly from the IRS, which meant that whoever disclosed it was willing to commit a federal crime punishable by up to five years in prison. When NOM tried to obtain the names of those who had access to their IRS documents, the IRS gave NOM representatives an *Alice in Wonderland* response: the same law that prohibited disclosing their confidential tax returns also prevented them from disclosing information about who had disclosed them!

Case Files and Casuistry

The IRS scandal broke because tax lobbyist Celia Roady asked a planted question of Lois Lerner at the 2013 meeting of the American Bar Association Section of Taxation's Exempt Organizations Committee (ABA EO). It's worth noting that the minutes for this May 10, 2013, ABA EO meeting are not yet available and – given what may have been said there about going after Tea Party groups – may never be made available.

The ABA EO meets three times a year. The committee has over 500 members, who are mostly tax attorneys, law students, and lobbyist insiders. These meetings serve as a sort of demilitarized zone, where high-profile lawyers who want their clients to pay fewer taxes meet government officials who want those high-profile lawyers' jobs down the line.

The planted question Celia Roady asked came four days before George, the IRS inspector general for tax administration, was to deliver the report on the targeting of conservative groups his unit had been working on for over a year. The IRS wanted to get out ahead of the firestorm it was sure to ignite. In the question-and-answer period after Lerner's speech, Roady asked about concerns that reviews of applications for nonprofit status from Tea Party organizations were taking too long. Pretending she was reacting spontaneously while in fact reading from a piece of paper, Lerner said that the agency had been experiencing a big uptick in applications and was backlogged. Then she said that agents in Cincinnati had used search terms like *Tea Party* and *patriots* in subjecting applications to undue scrutiny. She also acknowledged that the IRS had sent follow-up letters in some cases asking for inappropriate information about organizations' aims and backers. She also said that it was an internal problem in the Cincinnati office.

The firewall position – that this was Cincinnati-centric – was doomed to erode from the start. In the original e-mails between the Cincinnati office and Holly Paz, the Washington-based IRS supervisor, regarding the "be on the lookout" list, the "inappropriate criteria" that trigger special attention are described by John Shafer, the Cincinnati group manager:

> *The following are issues that could indicate a case to be a potential "tea party" case and sent to Group 7822 for secondary screening.*
>
> *1. "Tea Party", "Patriots", or "9/12 Project" is referenced in the case file.*
>
> *2. Issues include government spending, government debt, and taxes.*
>
> *3. Educate the public through advocacy/legislative activities to make America a better place to live.*

4. Statements in the case file that are critical of how the country is being run.

What this list really means is that those who call themselves patriots, who hold the founders' views on politics, and who want to better educate the public are now threats. In short, we've gone from "dissent is patriotic" to "dissent is worthy of an audit."

A Note to Investigators: The IRS Paper Trail

How can Congress effectively investigate and deal with the IRS scandal? Follow the paper.

The agency, as I've said, is highly computer-automated. Status numbers, specialist codes, and group numbers are all searchable. With audit trails, it should have been easy to identify who had access to the "Tea Party" case files. So why didn't the inspector general for tax administration check who handled the cases when completing its report? Could it have been that the inspector general was meant to hide the real culprits?

Another place to investigate are the changes made in the IRS's manual (IRM). On May 15, 2013, five days after Lois Lerner answered Celia Roady's planted question, IRM Section 4.76.4 (exempt organizations examination guidelines for private foundations) received a complete revision by Lerner. Given Lerner's past chicanery, those revisions warrant a careful examination. Coincidentally, May 15 was the same day that IRS Commissioner Steven Miller resigned and President Obama called the targeting of conservative groups "inexcusable." Even after three months, we still don't know what material was removed, and, given the pace of the investigation, we may never.

Oversight, Investigations, and Accountability

The IRS scandal could have been prevented, and I could have helped prevent it. A year before the news broke of the targeting, I was approached by a Tea Party activist who alleged that the IRS was cracking down on conservative groups. The story appeared too fanciful, too Machiavellian, and too complex for the general readers I write for, so I let it go. But every word of it has since been proved true. Nor was I the only journalist this activist had approached or the only one who rejected it. The Republican-controlled Congress, too, ignored the complaints of Tea Party groups.

This tale has confirmed to me what I have long observed: conservatives do a terrible job of investigating the Washington bureaucracy, and the media of the right are largely reactive to whatever is going on in Congress or in the mainstream media.

This must change. Conservatives ought to investigate every aspect of how the IRS conducts itself and propose alternatives. While right-of-center think tanks have mastered the language of tax policy, they don't have a firm grasp on the personalities and philosophies behind tax-collecting policy. Until that changes, sloganeering about profoundly changing or even abolishing the IRS will be little more than empty words. The right's financiers and journalistic enterprises should invest seriously in understanding how the IRS functions and in looking for legislative solutions to curb its bad behavior.

The Republican-controlled Congress has the subpoena power. It should use it, if only to shame the tax collectors and slow them down. Special efforts should be made to discredit the idea that the IRS, however fearsome, is nonetheless a politically neutral body.

Conservatives should have little doubt that the IRS is hostile to them – explicitly so in a way that is more fundamental than its generally brutish behavior toward most individuals and organizations under its thumb. The IRS is much more tolerant of the left's clients certainly than to the organizations of the right that it persecutes. As this Broadside goes to press, for instance, the IRS has de facto legalized gay marriage by allowing homosexuals who are married legally in the 13 states that allow same-sex marriage to file jointly. This move allows gays who were married in one of those 13 states to receive federal tax benefits even if they live in a state that does not recognize gay weddings. The new rule applies retroactively, even to homosexuals who were married abroad and have below-standard paperwork for their unions.

The IRS is also comparatively easygoing

Conservatives do a terrible job of investigating the Washington bureaucracy, and the media of the right are largely reactive to whatever is going on in Congress or in the mainstream media.

---

on the issue of fraud by illegal aliens, another group favored by the left. A recent audit report by the inspector general for the Social Security Administration found that Obama's IRS was reluctant to penalize employers who have illegal workers who consistently used

Social Security numbers that did not match their names. The IRS, according to the IG report, made a "policy decision" to "legalize illegal aliens" and wound up paying illegals $4.2 billion in refundable additional child tax credits in 2010 alone. In 2011, according to the inspector general for tax administration, the IRS would pay more than $46 million in tax refunds to what theoretically were 23,994 illegal aliens who used the same address in Atlanta. In 80 percent of the fraudulent cases, "unauthorized noncitizens" used Social Security numbers belonging to actual citizens.

At the same time, the IRS is harassing veterans groups, like the American Legion, by forcing their individual posts to provide official discharge papers and service records of members during the review of their tax-exempt status. "We've been fighting to get somebody's help for almost two years," said Bill West, the legion's adjutant for Texas.

So what must be done? Conservatives have rightly called for a simplified tax code that eliminates deductions, but policy alone won't solve the problem of the IRS. Reform must include recognizing that the soul of the IRS bureaucracy needs reshaping. If the abuses continue, the Tea Party – the target of the IRS's black operations – should ask itself if it really means what is says when it describes itself as "taxed enough already," and it should begin a movement to cut off the hand the IRS puts into the nation's pocketbook and around its neck.

First American edition published in 2013 by Encounter Books, an activity of Encounter for Culture and Education, Inc., a nonprofit, tax exempt corporation.
Encounter Books website address: www.encounterbooks.com

Manufactured in the United States and printed on acid-free paper. The paper used in this publication meets the minimum requirements of ANSI/NISO Z39.48–1992 (R 1997) (*Permanence of Paper*).

FIRST AMERICAN EDITION

LIBRARY OF CONGRESS
CATALOGING-IN-PUBLICATION DATA IS AVAILABLE

ISBN10 1-59403-744-2
ISBN13 978-1-59403-744-3
E-BOOK 978-1-59403-745-0

10 9 8 7 6 5 4 3 2 1

SERIES DESIGN BY CARL W. SCARBROUGH